MW00636493

WHAT ARE

MADE OF?

Written by Ruth Austin • Designed by Justine Edge

Dads like you are made of little things, gathered all together...

____

____

____

____

____

____

With love, ________________

It's not one unique quality or one special event that makes you the truly great dad you are. It's the example of fatherhood you put forward every day.

It's in the fleeting moments and the little actions, the small trials, the big triumphs, the shared jokes, the lack of sleep, and the fun. It's all that you're made of, all that you do and give—and it means so very much.

What are dads made of?

Sprinklings of laughter,
and mischief and calm,

Steady, gentle hands
and wide open arms.

Constant support,
and kindness and joy,

That's what dads
are made of.

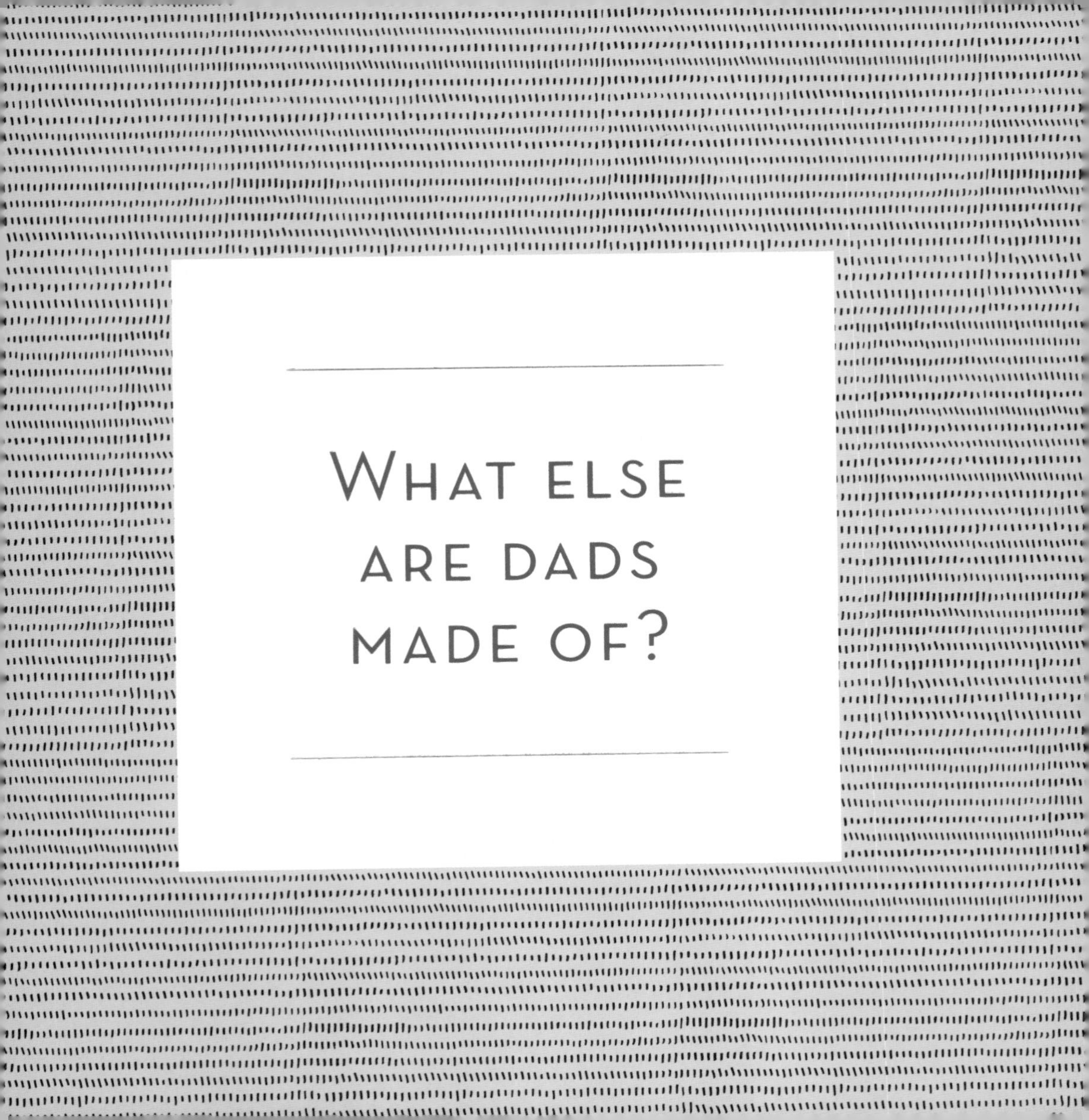
What else are dads made of?

A measure of values,
carefully taught,

Being woken too soon
and a few worried thoughts.

Bright wishes and dream
and a promise or two,

That's what dads
are made of.

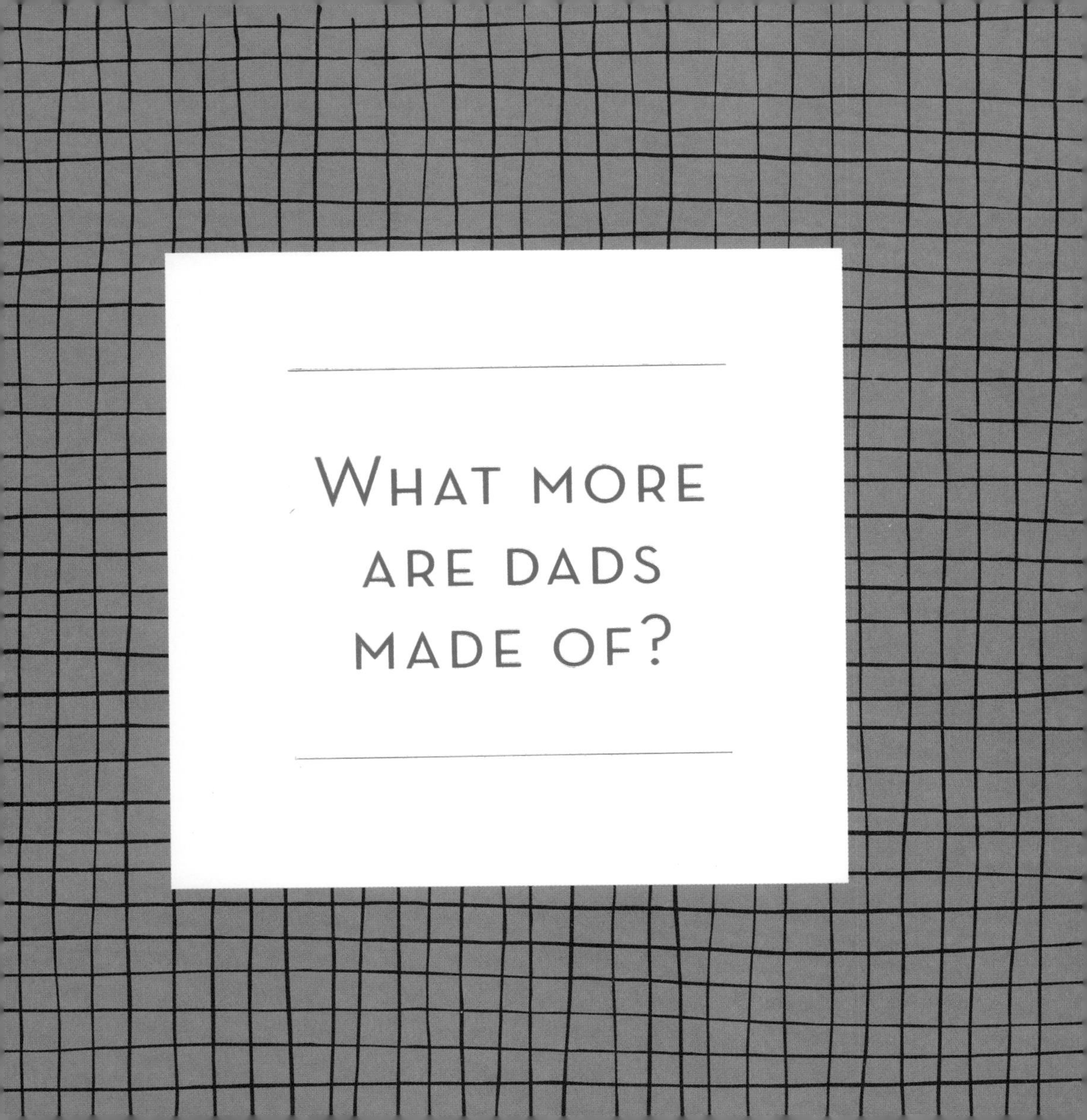
WHAT MORE
ARE DADS
MADE OF?

Bundles of guidance,
some patience that's tried,

Some learning to let go
and some wondering why.

A way of knowing to reach out,
without being told.

That's what dads
are made of.

What are dads really made of?

Tiny differences made
and small lessons shared,

Courage and affection,
dedication and care.

Always ready with comfort,
and a safe place to be,

That's what dads
are made of.

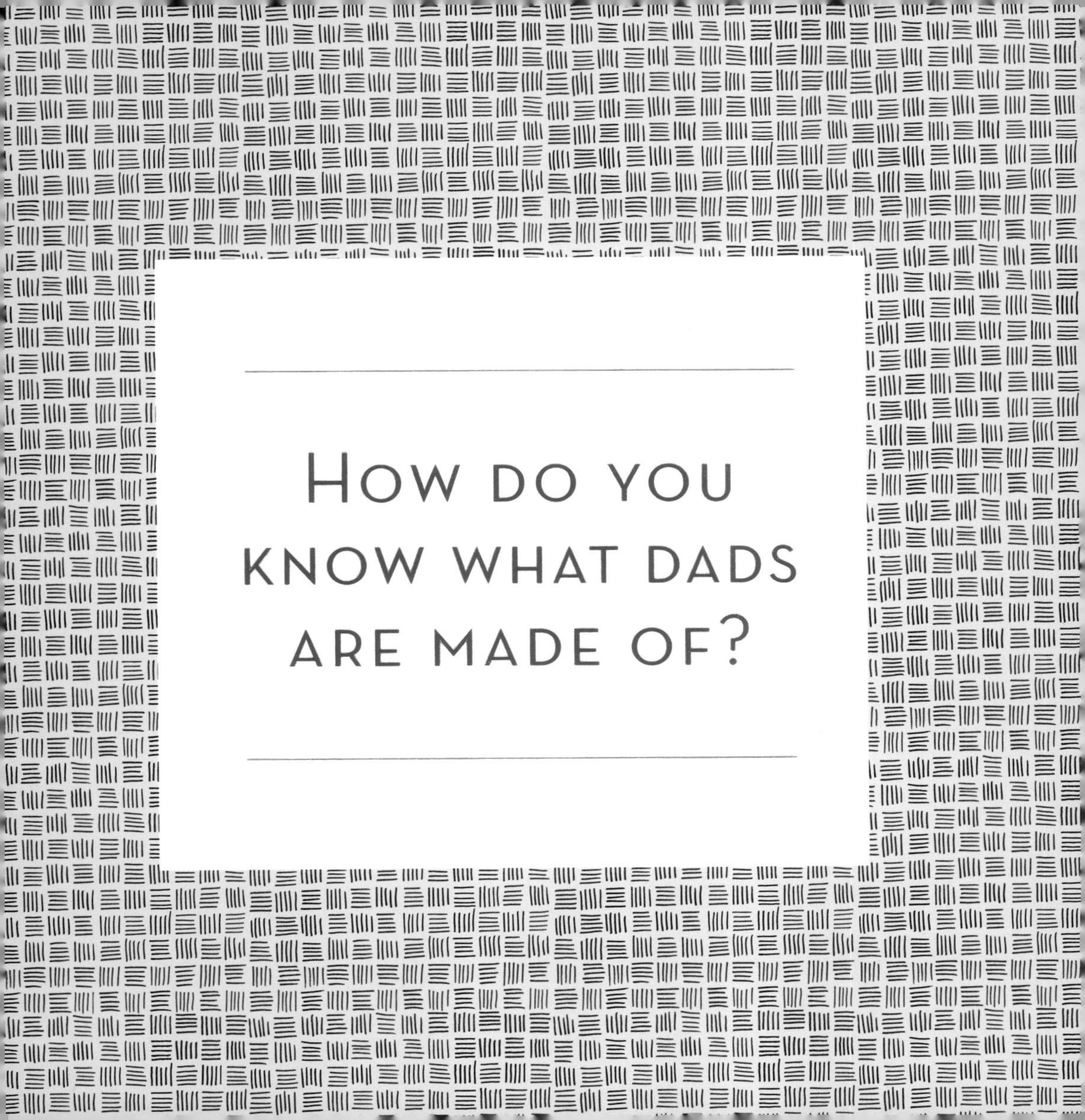
How do you know what dads are made of?

All the little efforts
and the time set aside,

A warm, tender smile
shining with pride.

The wholehearted attention.
The boundless love.

You're all the best things dads are made of.

With special thanks to the entire Compendium family.

CREDITS:

Written by: Ruth Austin
Designed by: Justine Edge
Edited by: Amelia Riedler

Library of Congress Control Number: 2017942875
ISBN: 978-1-943200-71-9

1st printing. Printed in China with soy and metallic inks.